HOW TO DRAW CUTE ANIMALS

by Martin Birch

THIS BOOK BELONGS TO

....

Table of Contents

WHAT DO WE NEED

F
H2
H1
HB
B
B2
B3
B4
B5
B6
B7
B8

To start our drawing adventure, we will need several pencils of different hardness. For sketching drawings we use hard pencils such as: F, H and HB, and for shading and underlining the contours of soft pencils: from B to B8. However, at the beginning of the adventure with drawing, an ordinary pencil will also do its job. For erasing sketches, a bread eraser is great, which is not as hard as ordinary erasers and does not damage the page like they are.

A calipers or a ruler with holes in the shape of circles may be useful to draw perfect circles. However, the best method is exercise. Try to draw circles in one place so that the resulting circle is equal. Each next one will be much better.

A varied color palette will be useful for your drawings. Whether you achieve a certain effect with crayons, markers or paints depends only on you and your preferences. Remember to pay special attention to the shadows when coloring the drawing. The color will always be darker in shaded areas.

TECHNICS

1. The following five pictures show how to draw a blue crayon in five easy steps. Each animal in the book is made in the same simple way. We start by drawing a straight line and draw two circles at its ends. In the next step, we draw side lines by connecting both circles.

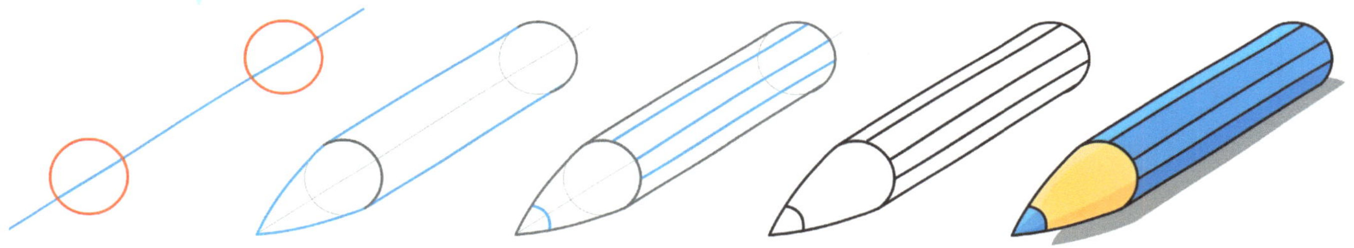

2. Note that when sketching your drawing, it will look slightly different than in the book (as shown in the five pictures below). Remember not to get discouraged. After all, it's training that makes perfect. Therefore, treat the drawing as a warm-up and the first exercise. Les't do!

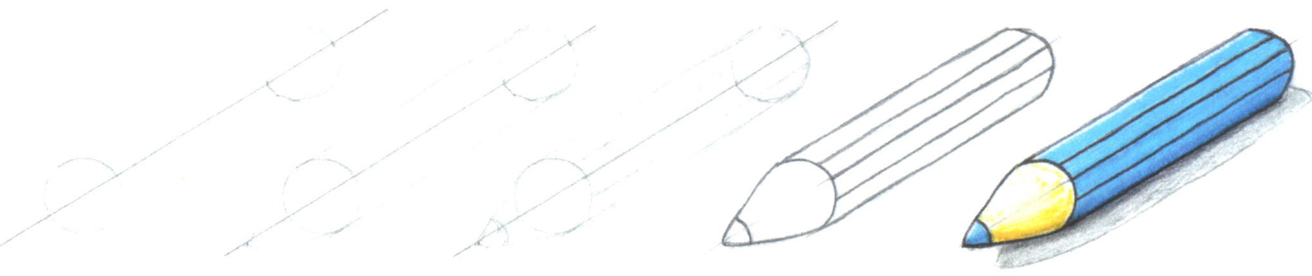

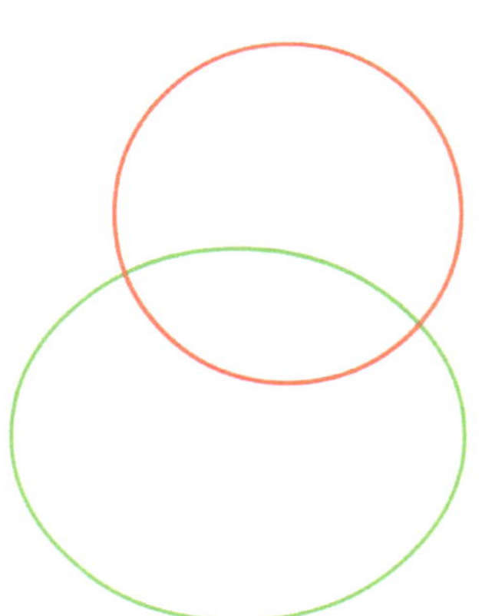

1. We start drawing the duck by sketching the oval (green). It will be on the torso. In the upper part of the oval we draw a circle (red). This will be the duck's head. The head is slightly shifted to the right of the body.

2. In the second step we can slightly erase unnecessary lines (in the picture it is a lighter gray line). At the bottom of the torso we sketch two ovals which will be the fins, and on the side one which will be the wing.

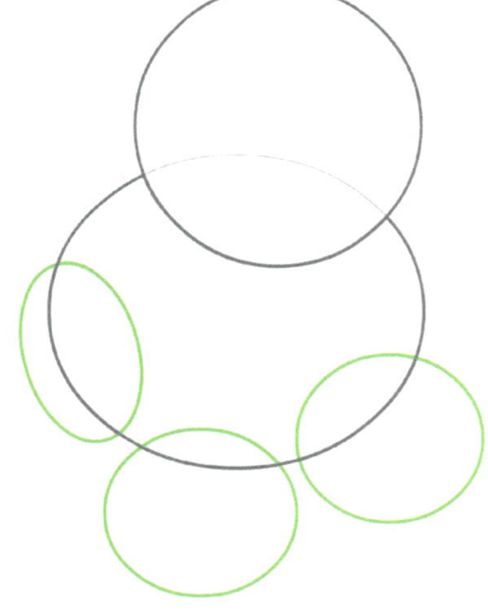

3. In the third stage, we do the same. We start by erasing unnecessary lines. We sketch the eyes in the upper circle. Note that one eye is perfectly round and the other is oval (this will give a 3D effect). Draw lines on the fins.

4. The next step is drawing the beak, which requires a bit more work from us. We give its upper part a wavy shape, and right below we draw two small circles, which will be the nose of the duckling.

5. At the end, erase all unnecessary auxiliary lines and correct the contours. Finally, color the drawing as shown in the picture, remembering about the shadows.

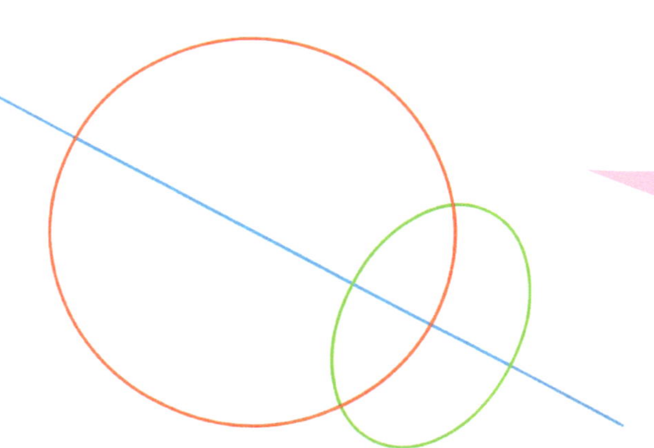

1. We drawing a straight auxiliary line (blue). In the center of the auxiliary line we sketch a large circle (red). It will be the torso. At the intersection of the circle and the auxiliary line, sketch an oval (green). It will be a pig's nose.

2. In the second stage we can slightly erase unnecessary lines (in the picture it is a lighter gray line). At the bottom of the torso, we sketch two ovals, which will be the legs. Inside the oval, the pig's nose, draw two more ovals, and above the nose, two small circles that will be the eyes.

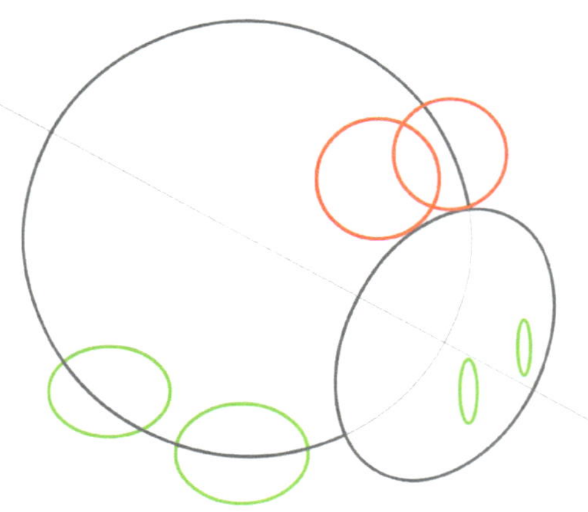

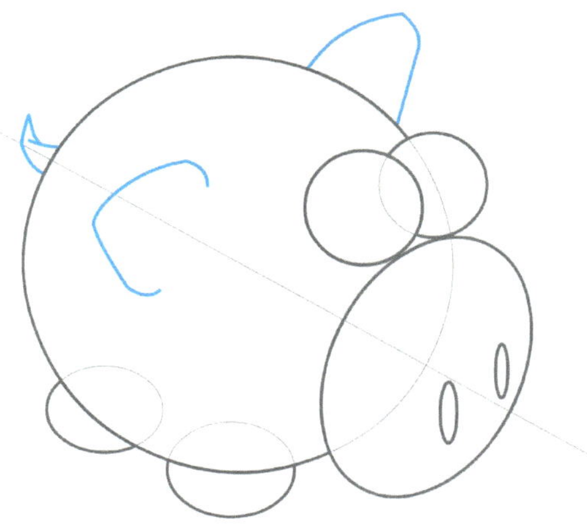

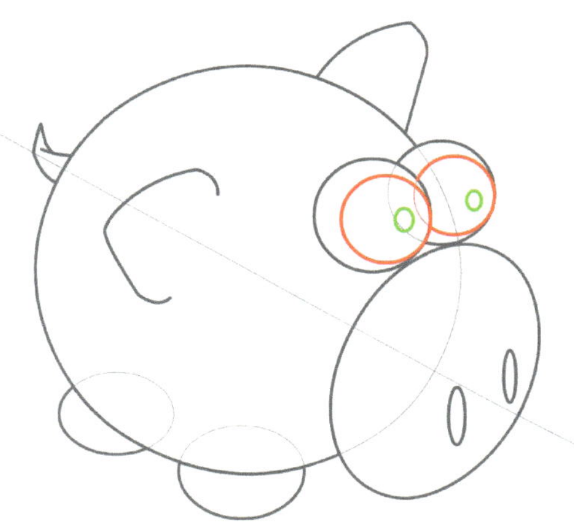

3. In the third stage, we proceed similarly, starting with erasing unnecessary lines. At the end of the torso, where the auxiliary line intersects, draw a petiole, and at the front of the torso, we draw pointed ears.

4. The next step is to carefully draw the eyes and eyelids. Remember to keep perspective.

5. At the end, erase all unnecessary auxiliary lines and correct the contours. Now color the drawing.

DOG

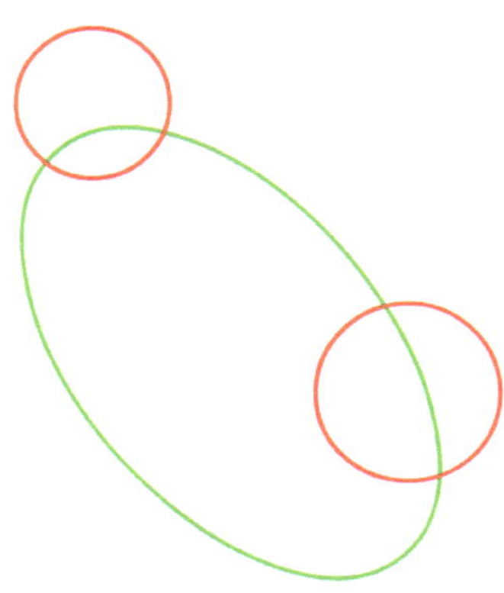

1. We start drawing the dog by sketching a large oval (green). It will be the head. At the top we sketch a circle (red) which will be the eye, and at the bottom of the torso another circle which will be the nose.

2. In the second stage, we can slightly erase unnecessary lines (in the picture it is a lighter gray line). Sketch the ear where the head meets the eye. We draw a slightly curved line where the nose meets the head. In the center of the upper circle, we sketch a smaller circle.

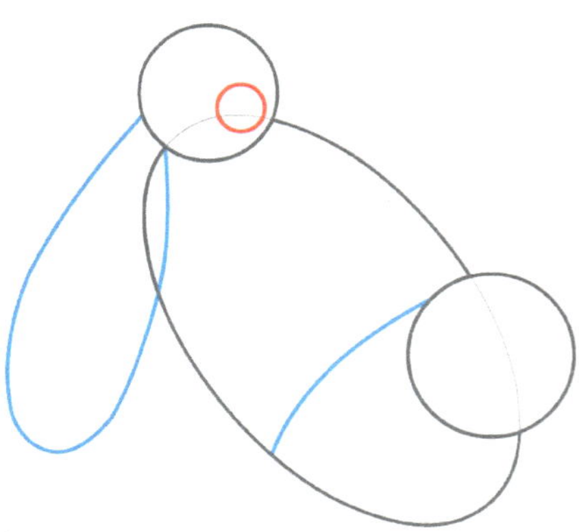

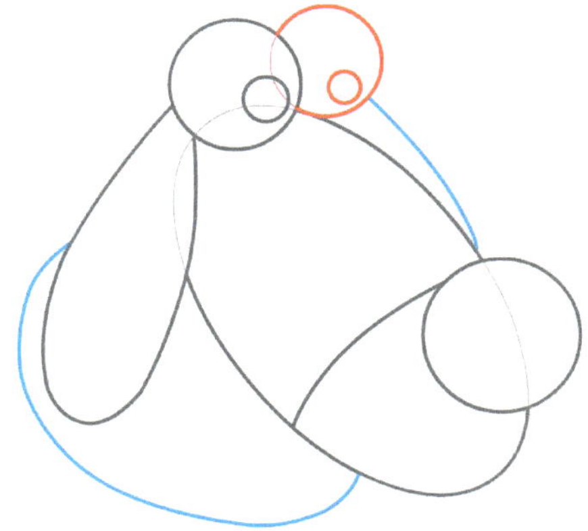

3. In the third stage, we proceed similarly, starting with erasing unnecessary lines. Then we sketch two circles at the top, so that the eyes are formed. Behind the upper circle we draw the outline of the second ear. Finally, we sketch the outline of the torso.

4. The next step is to draw slightly arched lines in the place of the eyes, so that the eyelids are formed. Sketch the tail at the end of the body, and three ovals at the bottom, which will be the legs. In the center of the head, we can draw a few arched lines that will be the eyelids.

5. At the end, erase all unnecessary auxiliary lines and correct the contours. Now color the drawing as in the picture, remember about the shadows.

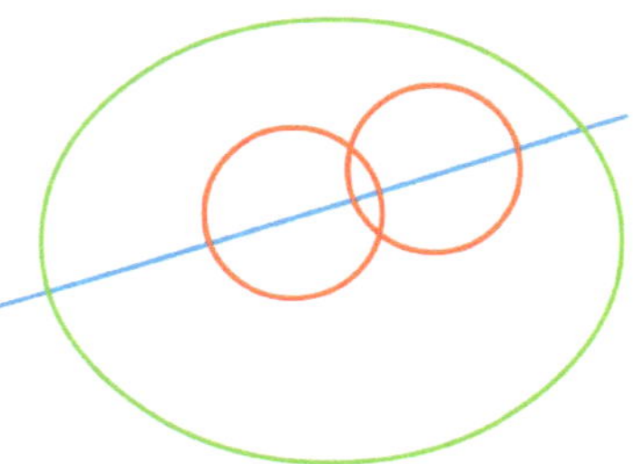

1. We start drawing the frog by sketching an auxiliary line (blue). In the center of the auxiliary line we draw two circles (red), which will be the eyes of the frog. Then we draw a large oval (green) so that the auxiliary line cuts it in half.
This will create the frog's head.

2. In the second step we can slightly erase unnecessary lines. (It is the lighter gray line in the image). Inside the two circles, we sketch more circles so that the eyelids and eyes of the frog are formed. Under the eyes, we sketch two ovals that will be the nose. Then sketch the smile and slightly round the head (blue).

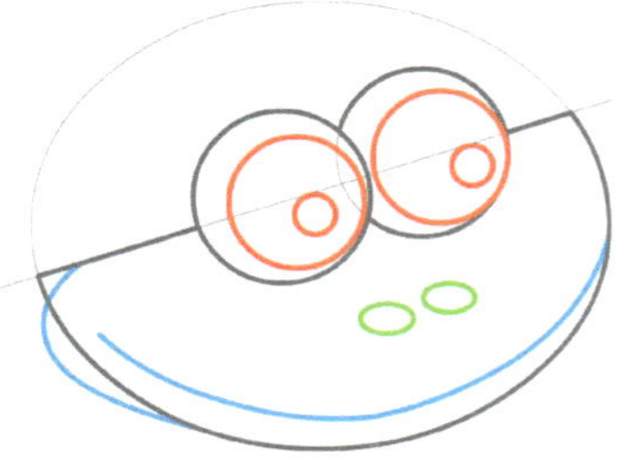

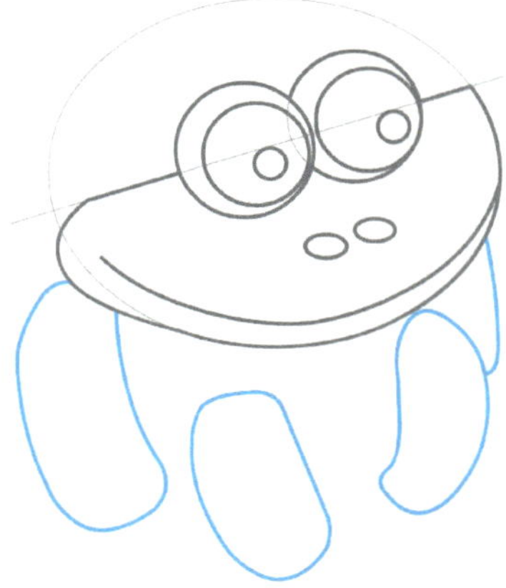

3. In the third stage, we proceed similarly, starting with erasing unnecessary lines. Sketching the frog's legs will be a bit more difficult task. Remember that we only see the outline of the hind leg.

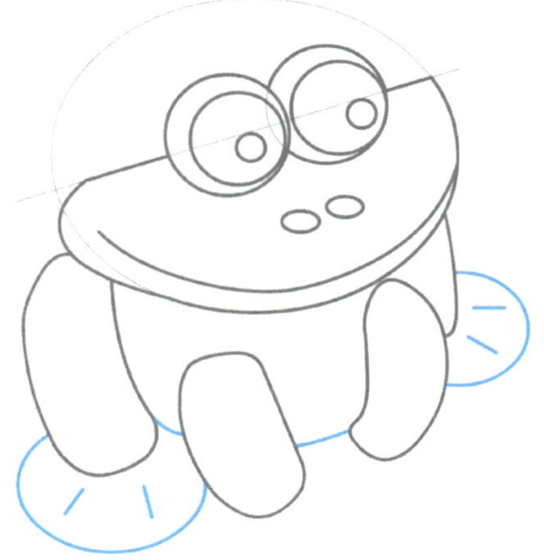

4. The next step is to connect the paws with slightly arched lines, so that the outline of the torso is formed. Then we sketch the fins.

5. At the end, erase all unnecessary auxiliary lines and correct the contours. Now you can color it like in the picture, remembering about the shadows.

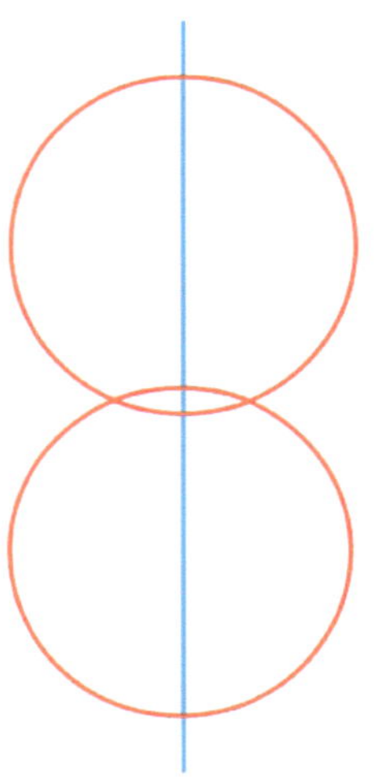

1. We drawing a simple auxiliary line (blue). In the center of the extension line, we sketch two circles (red). The circles should slightly overlap. The top circle will be the teddy bear's head and the bottom circle will be the teddy bear's body.

2. In the second step, we can slightly erase unnecessary lines (in the picture it is a lighter gray line). On the upper circle, we sketch the ears of the teddy bear. We draw two small circles successively, the teddy's eyes, and a slightly arched line below (which will mark the teddy's mouth).
We sketch the outline of the teddy's paw along the body.

3. In the third stage, we proceed similarly, starting with erasing unnecessary lines. Then we finish drawing the ears. We copy their shape and draw them in the middle on a slightly smaller scale. We draw two small circles inside the eyes, and a slightly larger circle under the eye line. We draw the shape of the mouth and paws. At the bottom we draw the lower paw.

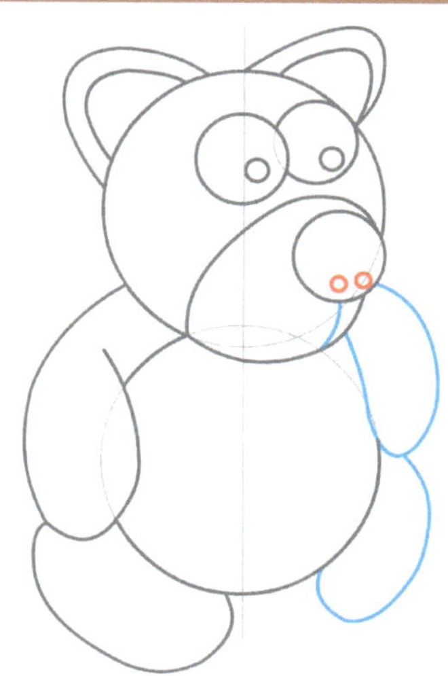

4. The next step is to draw two small circles inside the nose and a small line under it. Sketch the paws on the right.

5. At the end, erase all unnecessary auxiliary lines and correct the contours. Now color it as in the picture, remembering about the shadows.

1. We drawing a straight auxiliary line (blue). In the upper part of the auxiliary line, we draw an oval (green), which will be the giraffe's head. In the lower part of the auxiliary line we draw a slightly larger oval, which will be the body.

2. In the second step, connect the torso to the head, drawing the neck along the auxiliary line. At the bottom of the torso, we sketch the three legs of the giraffe. The fourth leg is invisible because we draw in perspective.

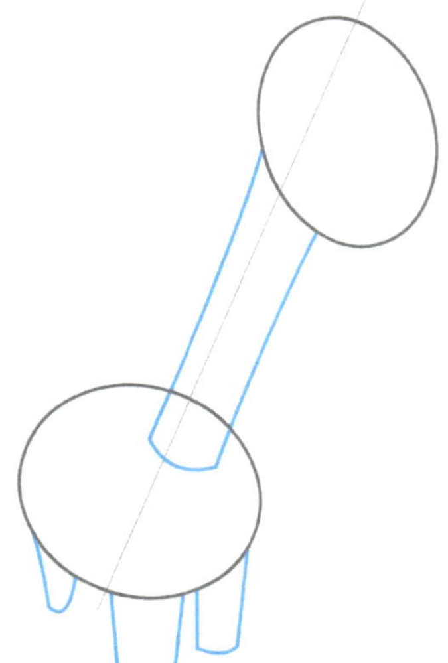

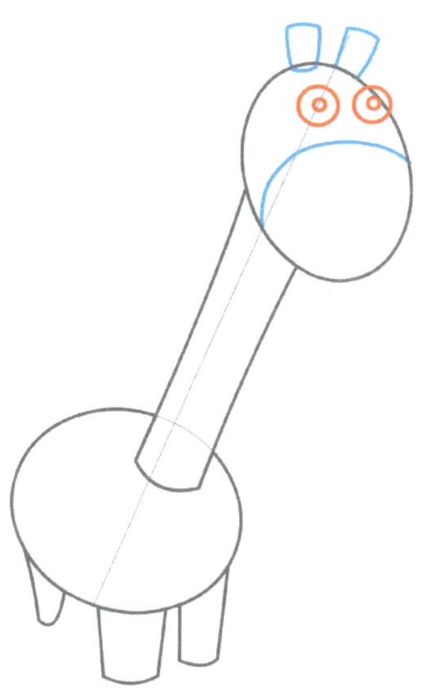

3. In the third stage, we can slightly erase unnecessary lines. We draw horns on the head and eyes a little lower. At the bottom of the head, we draw a slightly arched line so that a snout is formed.

4. The next step is to draw the ears. One ear is whole, the other ear is only a fragment. Below the line that separates the face from the head, we draw a nose. Finally, we draw patches: from smaller ones on the neck to larger ones on the body.

5. At the end, erase all unnecessary auxiliary lines and correct the contours. Now color the drawing as shown in the picture, remembering about the shadows.

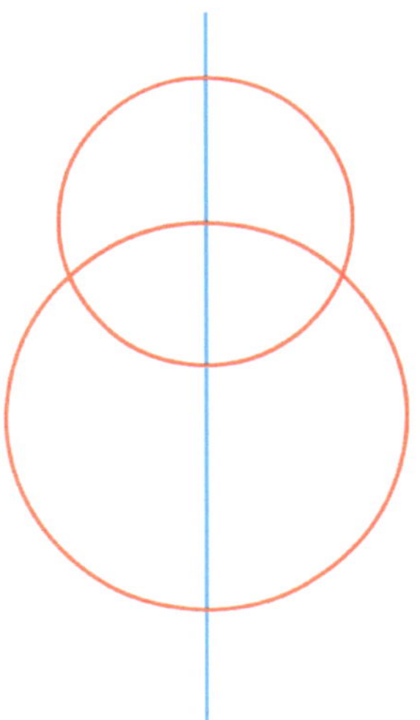

PENGUIN

1. We drawing a simple auxiliary line (blue). Then, on the auxiliary line, we sketch two circles (red). Notice that the top circle is smaller and the bottom circle is larger. The top one will be the head of the penguin and the bottom one will be the body.

2. In the second stage, we can slightly erase unnecessary lines (in the picture it is a lighter gray line). Then, on the sides of the torso, sketch the wings (blue). In the lower part of the torso, we draw two ovals, which will be the penguin's fins.

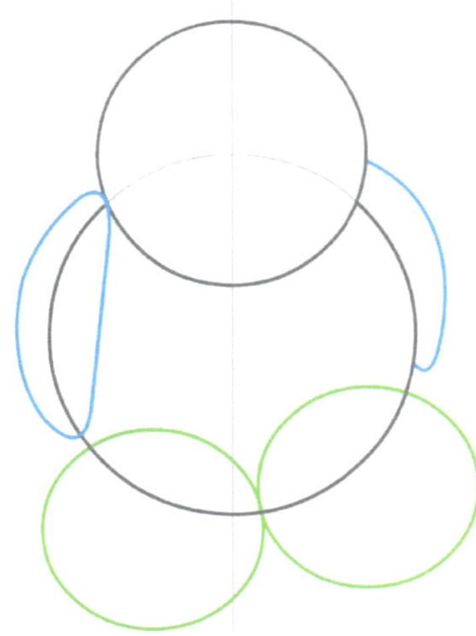

3. In the third stage, we proceed similarly, starting with erasing unnecessary lines. Then we sketch the eyes. Notice that one eye is exactly in the center of the head. We draw the beak below, starting with sketching the circle.

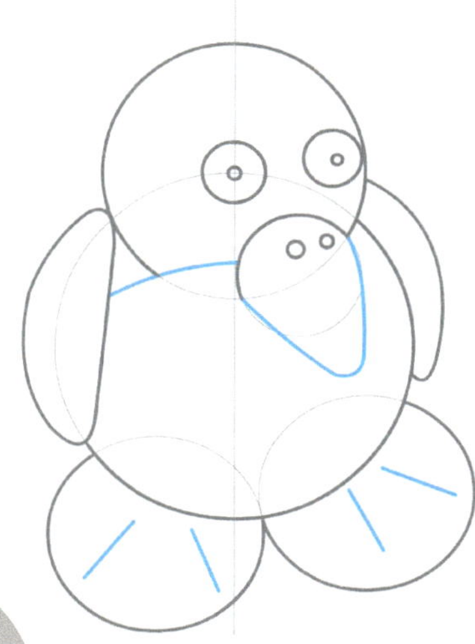

4. The next step is to sketch the bow. We draw its shape to the previously sketched circle. Then we draw one slightly curved line from the wing towards the bow and draw straight lines on the fins.

5. Finally, erase all unnecessary auxiliary lines and correct the contours. Now color the drawing as shown in the picture, remembering about the shadows.

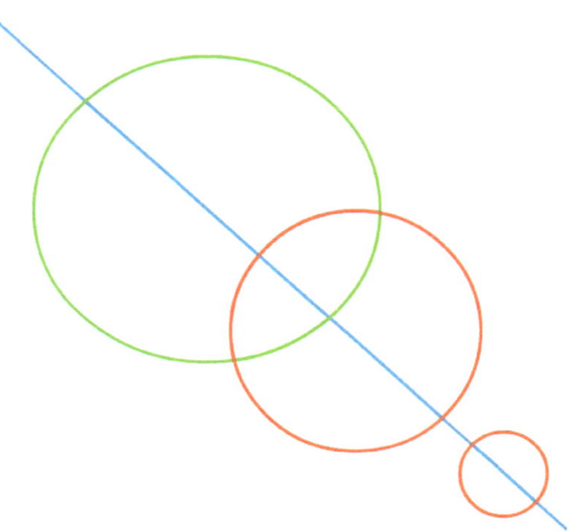

1. We drawing a straight auxiliary line (blue). Then we sketch on the auxiliary line two large and small circles (red) and one oval (green). The body of the mouse is made of the oval and the head of the large circle. The smaller circle that will form the nose is slightly further from the head.

2. In the second stage we can slightly erase unnecessary lines (in the picture it is a lighter gray line). Then we connect the head and nose with two straight lines (blue). On the upper part of the head, we sketch four circles so that the eyes are formed. In the lower part of the torso we draw two ovals from which the paws will be formed.

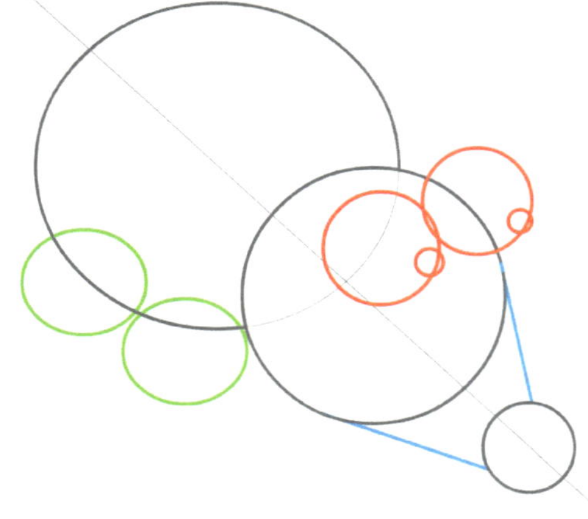

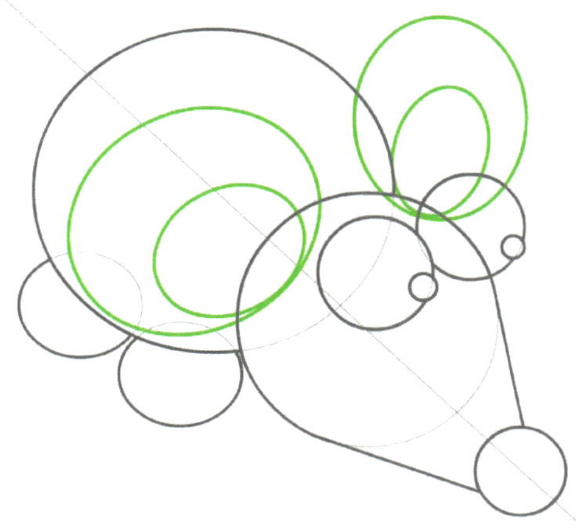

3. In the third stage, we proceed similarly, starting with erasing unnecessary lines. Then we sketch four ovals so that the ears are formed.

4. The next step is to sketch the eyelids on the eyes and the tail. Additionally, we can draw three small circles on the head instead of a mustache.

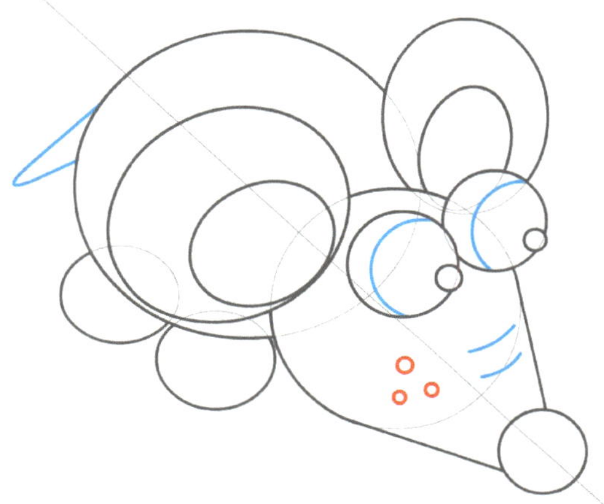

5.At the end, erase all unnecessary auxiliary lines and correct the contours. Now color the drawing as shown in the picture, remembering about the shadows.

1. We drawing two ovals, which will form the body (green). In the upper part of the first one, we sketch two circles, i.e. the eyes of the snail (red).

2. In the second stage, we draw lines to the previously sketched ovals (blue). Then we draw the eyelids and another two small ovals so that the eyes of the snail are formed.

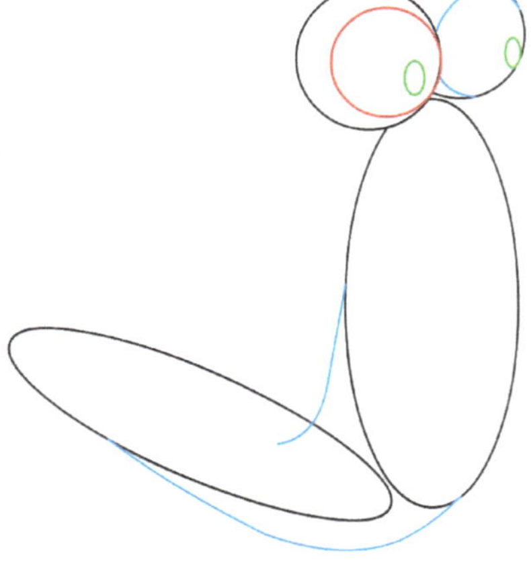

3. We start the third stage by sketching two ovals - one large and one smaller. They will form a shell (green). Then we sketch a small circle, and on the other side the lines (blue).

4. The next step is to draw the mouth, a line in the middle of the mouth and finish the snail house.

5. Finally, erase all unnecessary auxiliary lines and correct the contours. Now color the drawing as shown in the picture, remembering about the shadows.

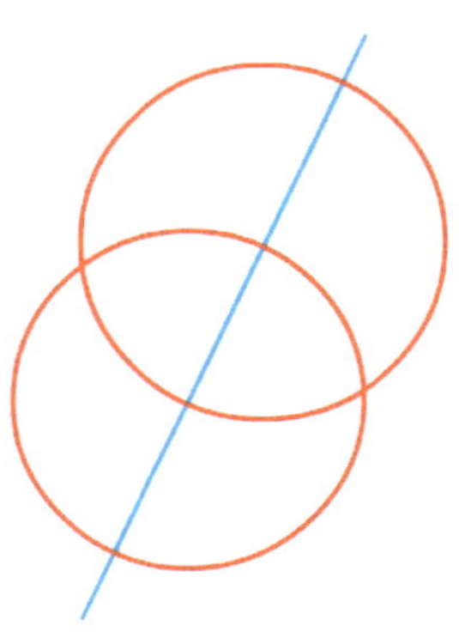

1. We drawing a straight auxiliary line (blue). Then we sketch two circles on the auxiliary line (red). Notice that the circles are overlapping each other. They will turn into a hippo's head.

2. In the second stage we can slightly erase unnecessary lines (in the picture it is a lighter gray line). Then we draw four circles (red). Two circles will be eyes, and the next two will be a hippo's nose. Next, we draw a smile and slightly enlarge the face (blue).

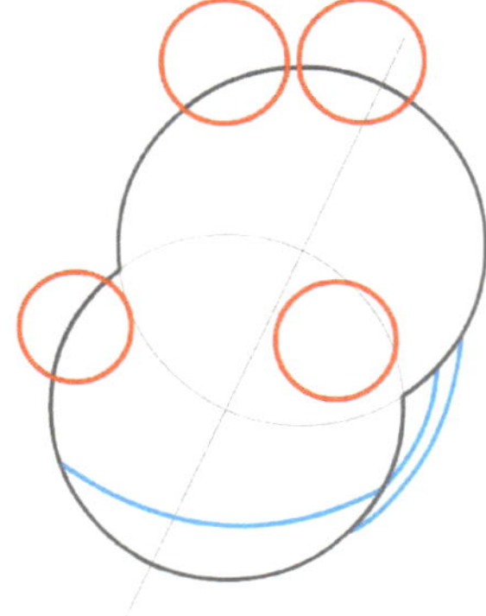

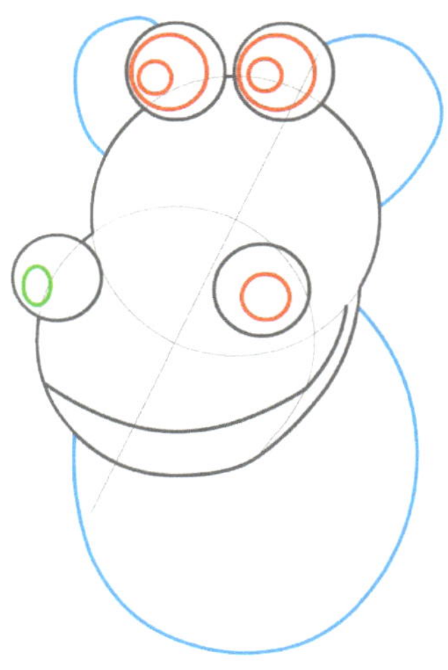

3. In the third stage, we can slightly erase unnecessary lines. We draw ears on the head, eyes a little lower. In the lower part of the head, we draw a circle and an oval one by one, so that the nose is formed. Then we sketch the torso.

4. The next stage is drawing the inside of the ears. Then we draw four ovals and add hippo's feet to the ovals. The next step is drawing teeth.

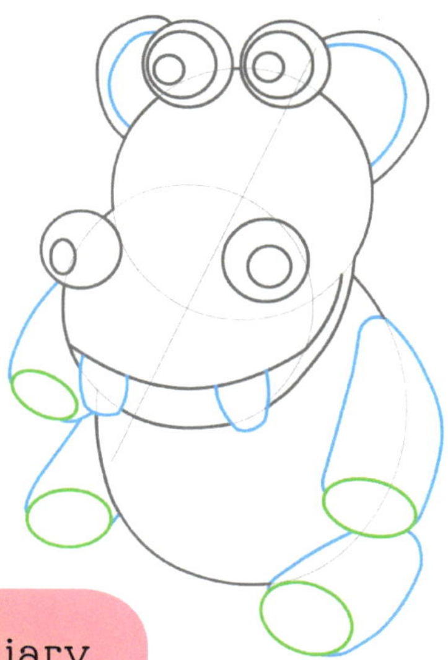

5. Finally, we erase all unnecessary auxiliary lines and correct the contours. Now color the drawing as shown in the picture, remembering about the shadows.

FISH

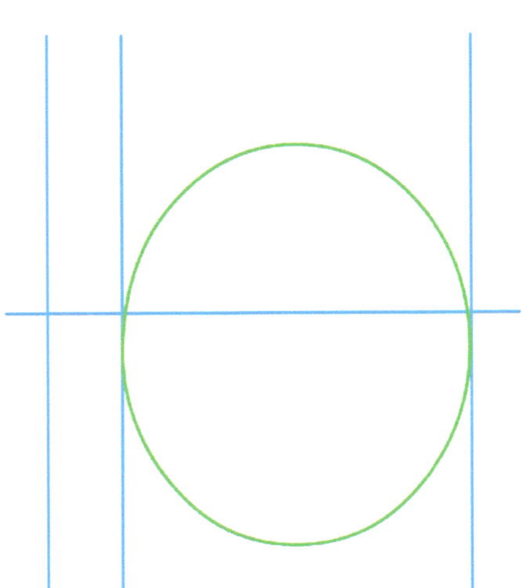

1. We start drawing the fish by drawing four simple auxiliary lines (blue). Between the auxiliary lines we draw an oval from which the body will be made (green).

2. In the next stage, we sketch the eyes. Notice that the oval eye is perfectly centered on the intersection of the extension lines. Then we sketch the faces with a line (blue) as shown in the picture. The next step is to draw the fin.

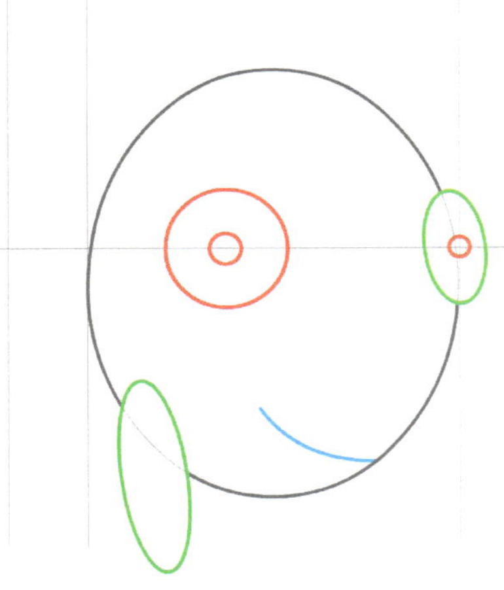

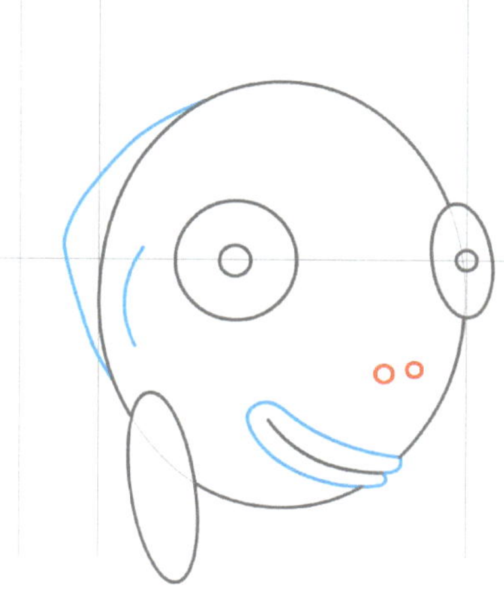

3. In the third stage, we can slightly erase unnecessary lines. Then we sketch and enlarge the outline of the torso. Successively we draw a short line so that the outline of the gills is formed, and then we outline the shape of the mouth. Additionally, we draw two small circles above the face.

4. The next step is to sketch the hind and upper fins. The rear fin should fit between the guidelines.

5. At the end, erase all unnecessary auxiliary lines and correct the contours. Now color the drawing as shown in the picture, remembering about the shadows..

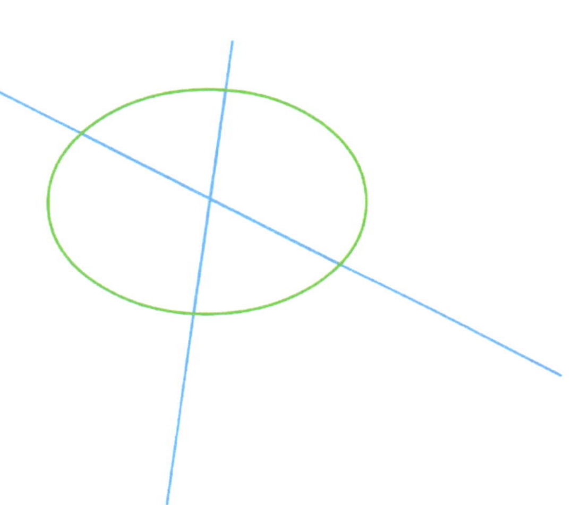

1.   We drawing two straight auxiliary lines (blue). The point where the auxiliary lines intersect is the center of the oval (green). It will be the body of the crab.

2. In the next stage, sketch the upper tongs. Once again, we can use auxiliary lines that mark the inner part of the pliers.

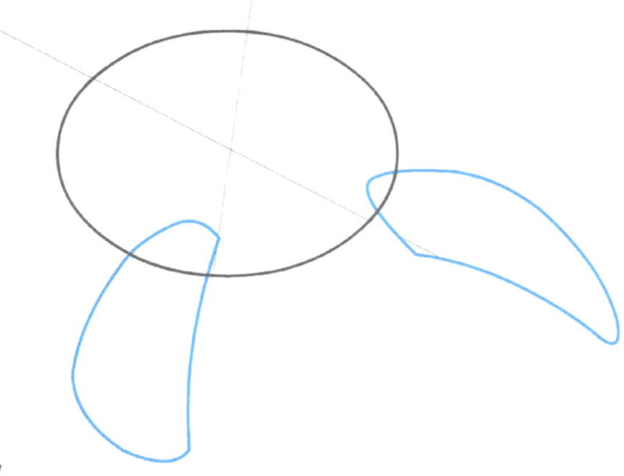

3. In the third stage, we can slightly erase unnecessary lines. Then in the center of the torso we sketch six circles from which the eyes will be formed. A little below we draw another two circles that will be the nose.

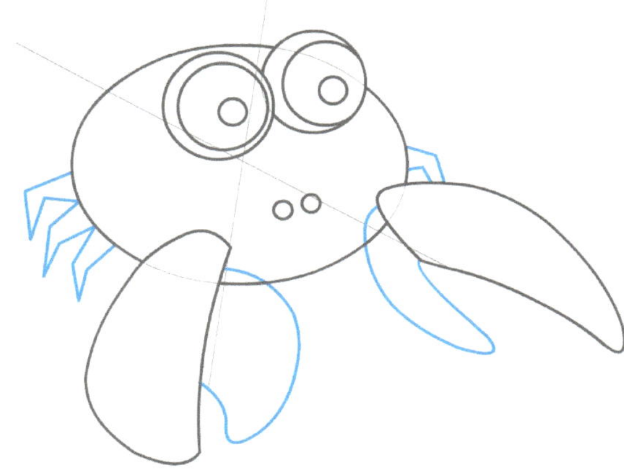

4. The next step is to sketch the legs. Then we draw the smaller crab claws. Note that they differ from each other, which is due to the perspective.

5. Finally, erase all unnecessary auxiliary lines and correct the contours. Now color the drawing as shown in the picture, remembering about the shadows.

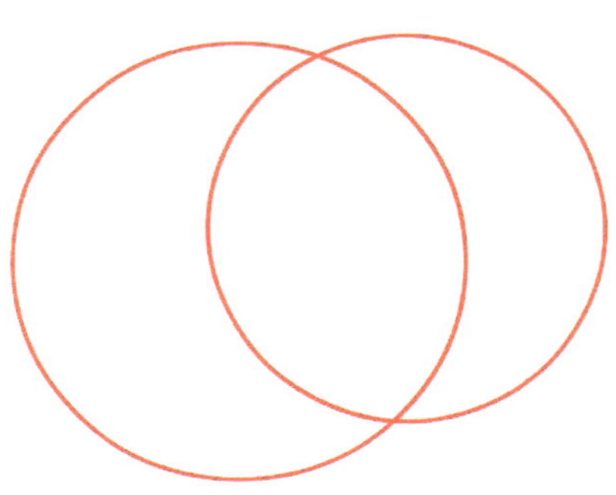

1. We start drawing the turtle by sketching two circles. Notice that the circles vary in size and overlap. The large circle will be the tortoise's shell and the smaller circle will be its head.

2. In the second stage we can slightly erase unnecessary lines (in the picture it is a lighter gray line). Then we draw the neck to the smaller circle, and under the large circle we sketch the lower part of the turtle's shell.

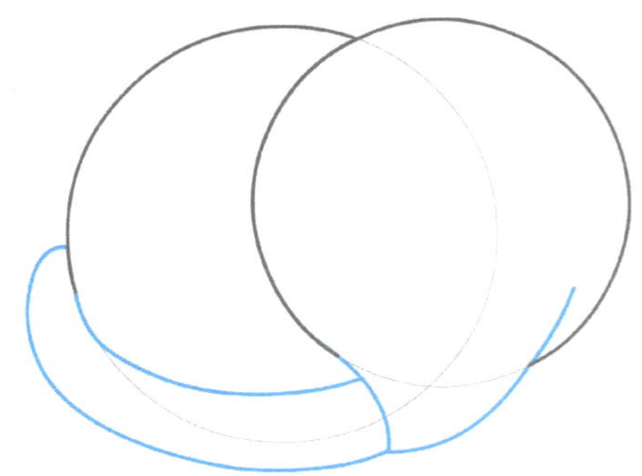

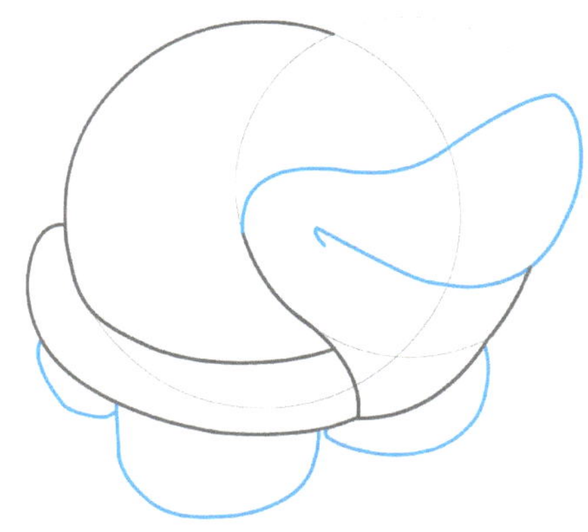

3. In the third stage, we can slightly erase unnecessary lines. Then we draw the faces of the turtle, this is a horizontal line on the oval of the head. Below the shell, we sketch the legs.

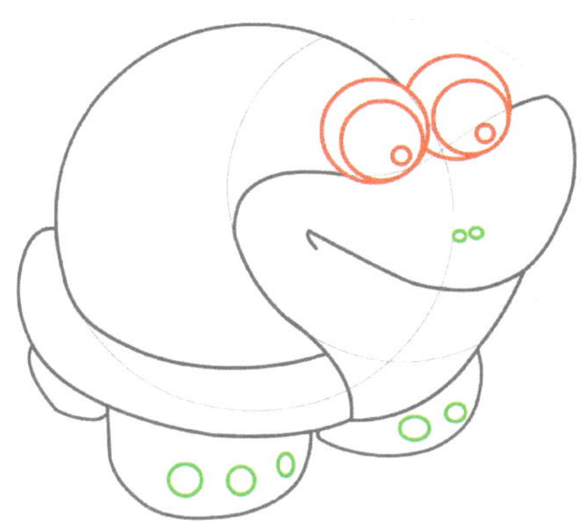

4. The next step is to sketch the eyes that are formed from six circles. We draw three circles for each eye, contained one in the other. In addition, we sketch ovals on the turtle's legs as its claws, and on its mouth, two small ovals from which the nose will form.

5. Finally, erase all unnecessary auxiliary lines and correct the contours. Now color the drawing as shown in the picture, remembering about the shadows.

1. We start by drawing a simple auxiliary line (blue). Then we sketch two circles on the auxiliary line (red). Notice that the guide line crosses their centers. The larger circle forms the center of the small circle with the extension line (at the intersection).

2. In the second stage we can slightly erase unnecessary lines (in the picture it is a lighter gray line). Then we sketch a part of the torso and extend the crocodile's head.

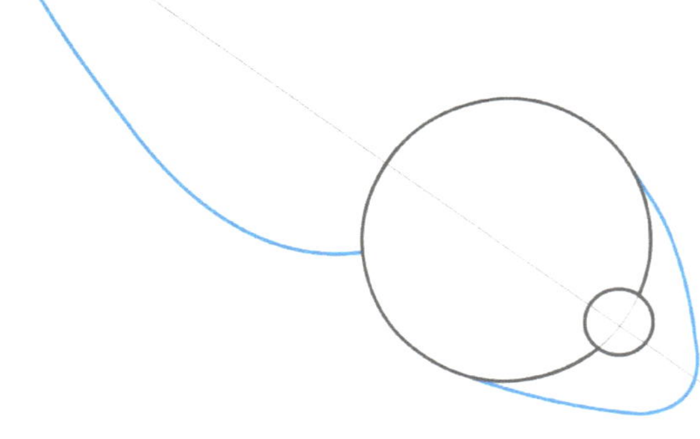

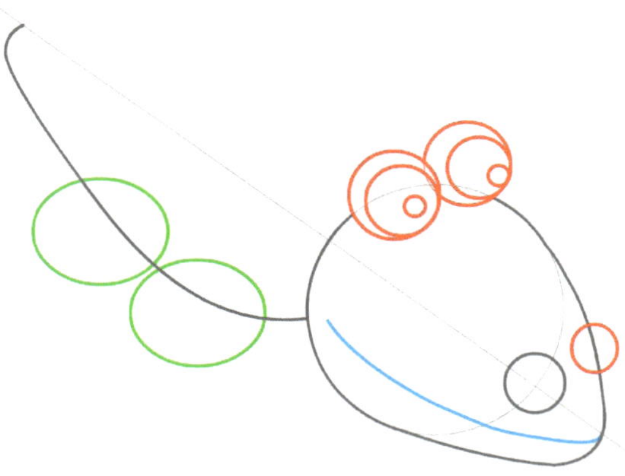

3. In the third stage, we can slightly erase unnecessary lines. Then we sketch the eyes, which consist of six circles. Sketch another circle on top of the crocodile's mouth, thanks to which the nose will be created. Sketch two ovals (green) under the body. Finally, we sketch a slightly arched line so that a crocodile smile appears.

4. The next step is to sketch the second half of the torso. In the place of the previously sketched ovals, we draw paws. On the line of the mouth we draw teeth and lines on the body.

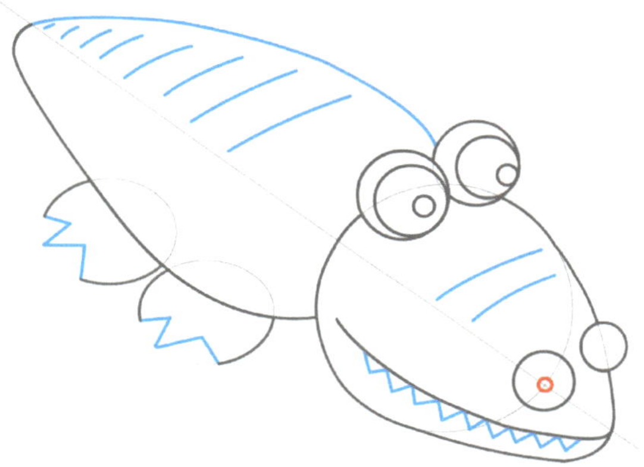

5. At the end, erase all unnecessary auxiliary lines and correct the contours. Now color the drawing as shown in the picture, remembering about the shadows.

1. We start drawing a seal by sketching a large circle (red). Then we sketch an oval (green) under it. They will form the body of the seal.

2. In the second stage, we can slightly erase unnecessary lines (in the picture it is a lighter gray line). Then we sketch the outline of the seal's body enlarging it (blue). Additionally, we sketch two circles in front of the torso, from which the front fins will be made.

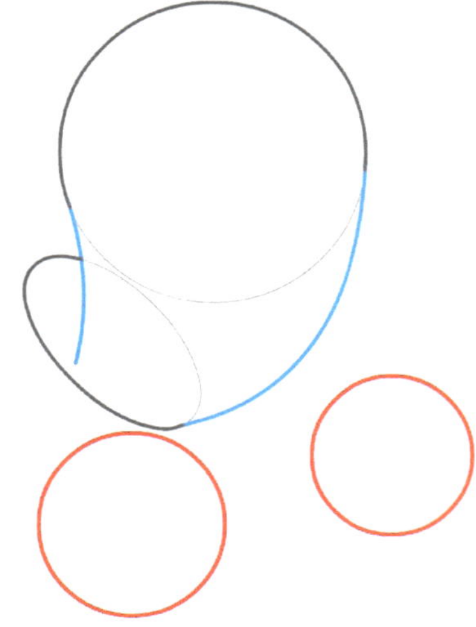

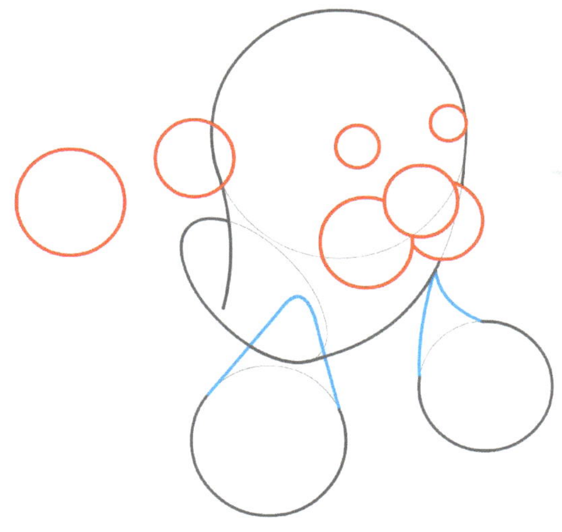

3. Now we can slightly erase unnecessary lines. Then we draw their outline (blue) to the front fins. Behind the torso we sketch two circles from which the rear fins will be formed. Then we sketch five circles in front. Two of them will be used to create the eyes, while the remaining ones will be used to make the face and nose.

4. The next step is to sketch the hind fins and complete the front fins. We add a few small circles on the mouth.

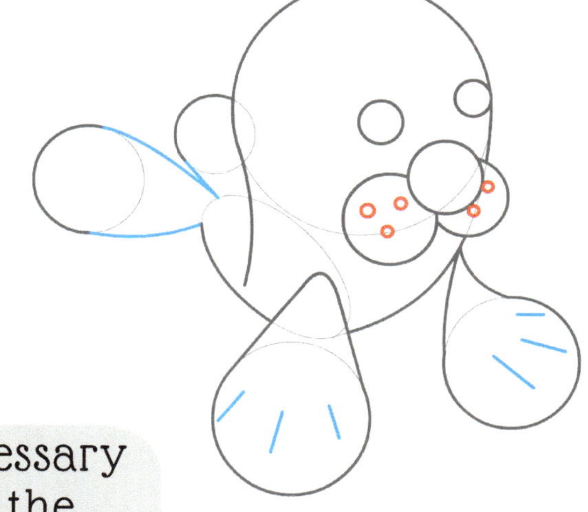

5. Finally, we erase all unnecessary auxiliary lines and correct the contours. Now color the drawing as shown in the picture, remembering about the shadows.

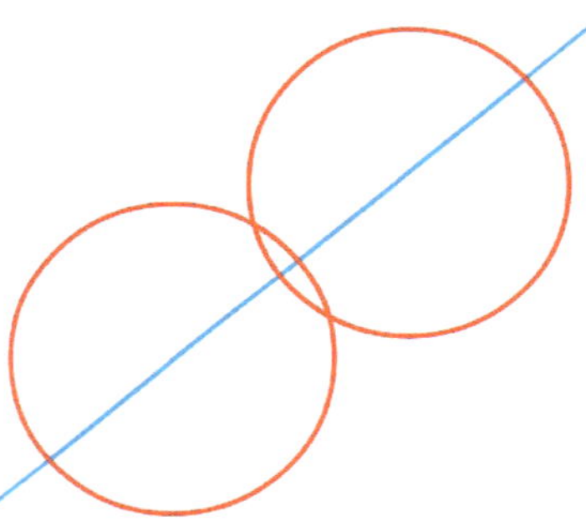

1. We start by drawing a simple auxiliary line (blue). Then we sketch two circles on the auxiliary line (red). Notice that the guide line crosses the centers of the circles and the circles overlap slightly.

2. In the second stage, we can slightly erase unnecessary lines (in the picture it is a lighter gray line). Then we sketch the outline of the elephant's ear and trunk (blue), as shown in the picture.

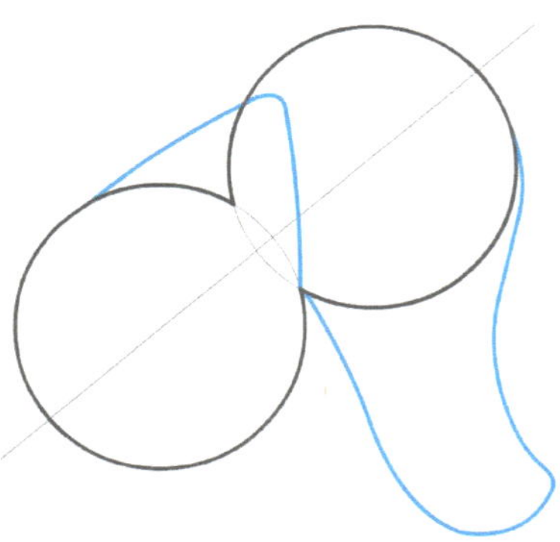

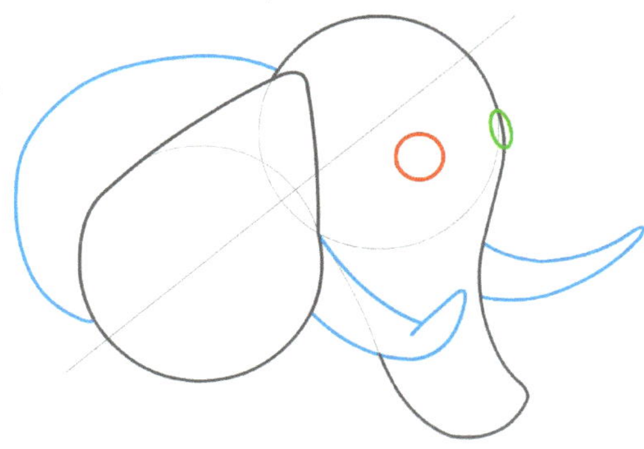

3. In the third stage, we can slightly erase unnecessary lines. Then we sketch the outline of the torso. Sketch the eyes on the elephant's head (red and green). Below the line of the head we draw the fangs.

4. The next step is to sketch the legs and tail. Additionally, we sketch circles on the legs (red) and lines on the ears and proboscis.

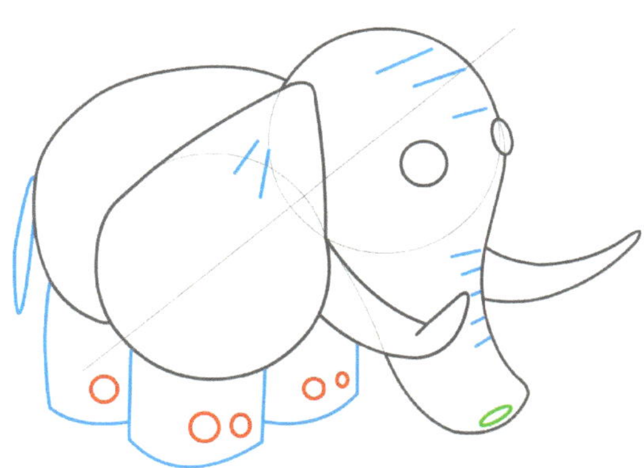

5. At the end, erase all unnecessary auxiliary lines and correct the contours. Now color the drawing as shown in the picture, remembering about the shadows.

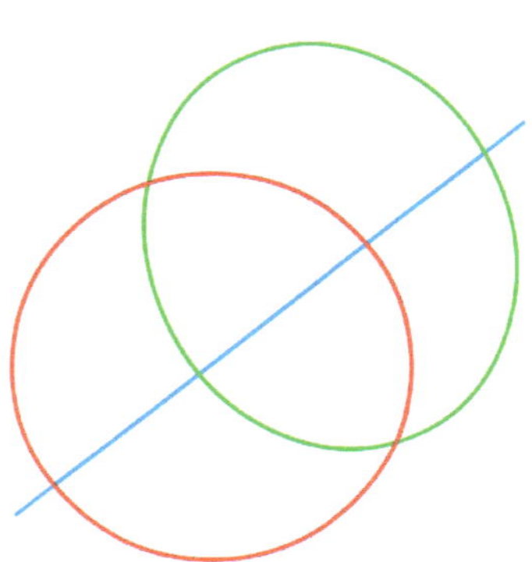

GORILLA

1. We start by drawing a simple auxiliary line (blue). Then we sketch a circle (red) and an oval (green) on it. Notice that the extension line intersects the center of the circle. The head of a gorilla will be made of the oval and the body will be made of the circle.

2. In the second stage we can slightly erase unnecessary lines (in the picture it is a lighter gray line). Then we sketch three circles (red) on the head. The middle one will be the nose and the other two eyes. Additionally, we sketch the outline of the gorilla's legs, which start at the head and extend beyond the circle of the body.

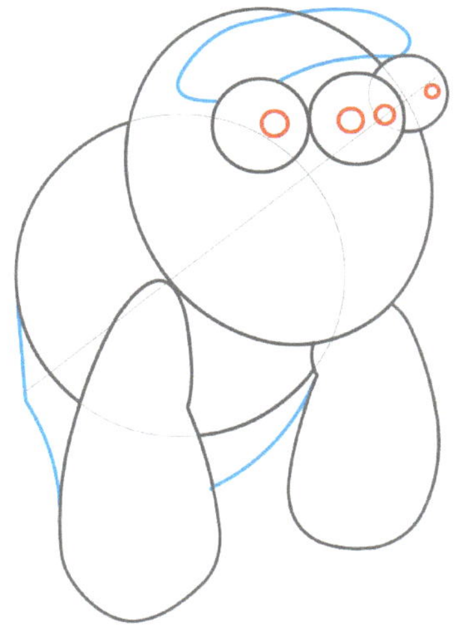

3. In the third stage, we can slightly erase unnecessary lines. Then we sketch the outline of the torso extending it. In addition, we sketch the forehead that is above the gorilla's eyes. We also draw four small circles to correct the eyes and nose.

4. The next step is to sketch the legs. Notice that the gorilla is sitting and the hind leg is almost invisible. Then we sketch the faces and delicately draw the eyelids as shown in the picture.

5. At the end, erase all unnecessary auxiliary lines and correct the contours. Now color the drawing as shown in the picture, remembering about the shadows.

MONKEY

1. We start by sketching two circles (red). Notice that the circles touch each other and are slightly offset from each other. The head of a monkey will be made from the upper circle and the body from the lower one.

2. Now we can slightly erase unnecessary lines (gray line). Then we draw two auxiliary lines in the upper circle. The top line will define the shape of the head and the bottom line will define the height of the eyes. A little below we sketch a circle that will be the nose (red). We slightly increase the outline of the body, and below we sketch two ovals (green), from which the paws will be formed.

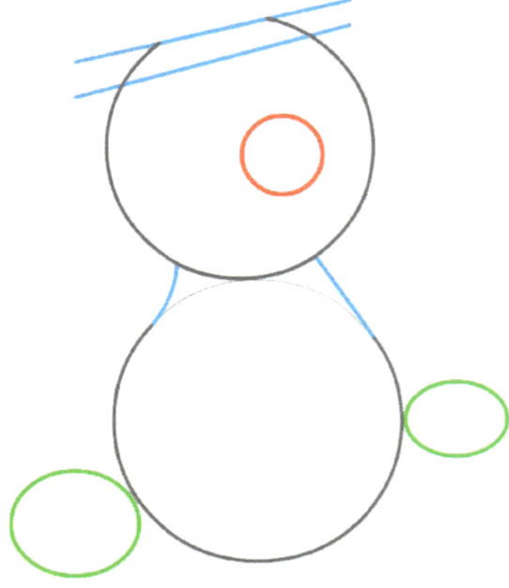

3. Now lightly erase the unnecessary lines. Then we sketch four circles so that the monkey's ears are formed. Below, we sketch another four circles to draw the eyes. From the nose line we draw the shape of the mouth, and then the outline of the paws. At the bottom of the torso we sketch two ovals (green) to draw the legs.

4. The next step is to reduce the shape of the head. Then we put a smile and a nose by drawing two circles (red). Then we sketch the monkey's tail and the belly lines on the body. We connect the lower ovals with two lines to create legs.

5. Finally, erase all unnecessary auxiliary lines and correct the contours. Now color the drawing as shown in the picture, remembering about the shadows.

1. We start by sketching two circles (red). Notice that the circles are overlapping and slightly offset from each other. The head of a panda will form from the upper circle, and the lower body from the lower one.

2. Now we can slightly erase unnecessary lines (gray line). Then, on the sides of the upper circle, we sketch two more, from which ears will be made, while in its center we draw two more circles to show patches. Below we sketch two ovals (green) from which the paws will be made. At the bottom of the torso, we sketch two circles. These will be her legs.

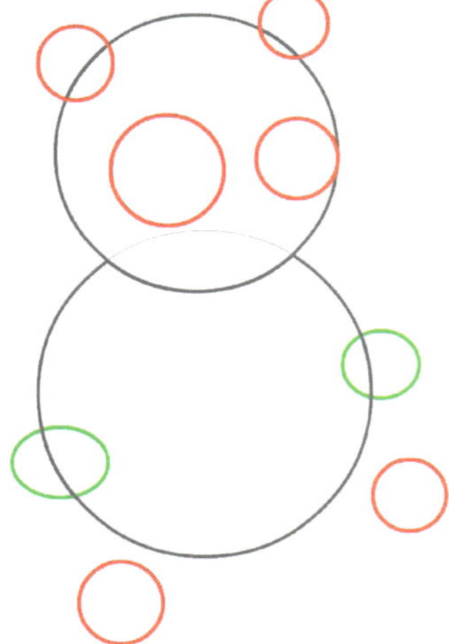

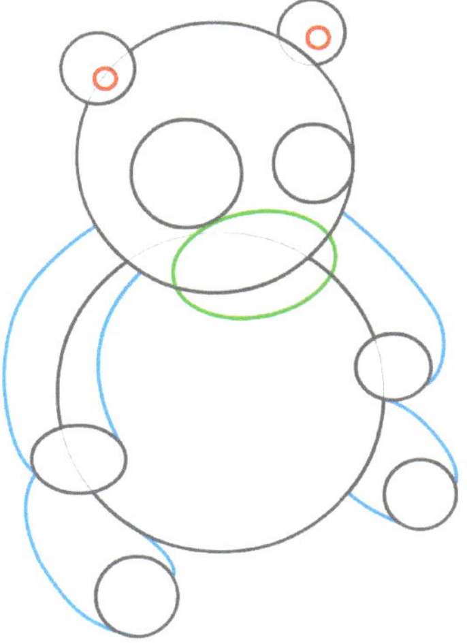

3. In the third stage, we can slightly erase unnecessary lines. Then we sketch two small circles in the ears. Below we sketch the oval (green). We draw lines to them, so that the paws and legs are created.

4. The next step is to draw the panda's face. It is made up of the eyes and mouth. First, we sketch a circle so that the panda's nose.

5. At the end, erase all unnecessary auxiliary lines and correct the contours. Now color the drawing as shown in the picture, remembering about the shadows.

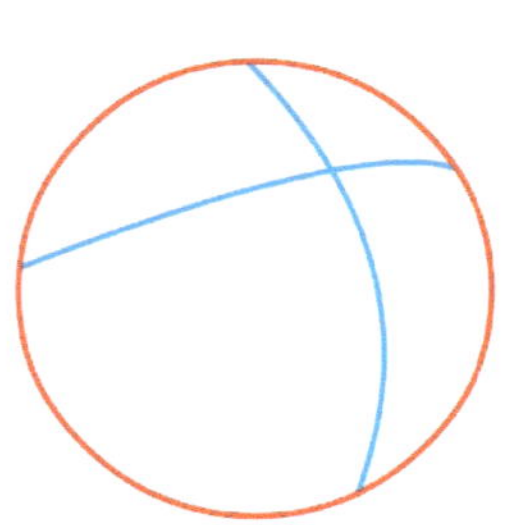

1. We start by sketching a circle (red). His head will also arise from the circle. Then two arcuate auxiliary lines (blue). The lines will mark the places where the eyes and nose are drawn.

2. Now, at the top of the circle, sketch the outline of the ears (blue). Then below, using the horizontal auxiliary line, we sketch his eyes. On the vertical auxiliary line we draw a small circle from which the nose will be made. A little below, we sketch another two circles that meet the nose. They will create a kitten's mouth.

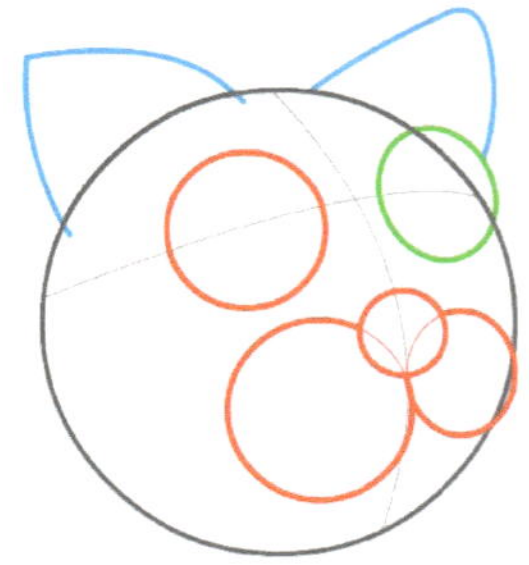

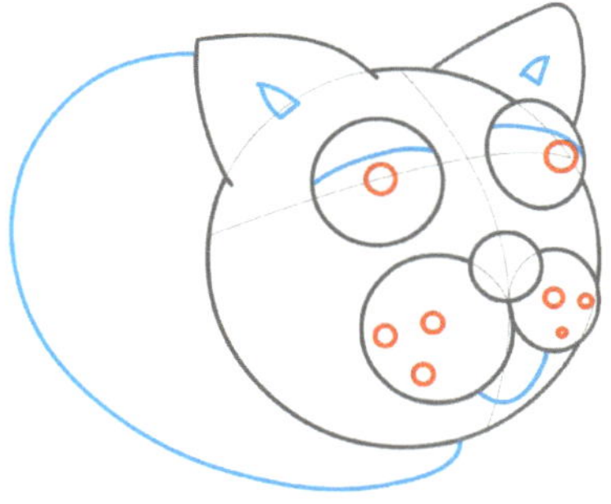

3. In the third stage, we can slightly erase unnecessary lines. Then we sketch the outline of the body, the inner part of the ears, eyelids and chin (blue). Below we draw eight circles (red).

4. The next step is sketching the feet and tail. Notice that the rear leg is tucked behind the front leg. We draw the tail as the last one.

5. Finally, erase all unnecessary auxiliary lines and correct the contours. Now color the drawing as shown in the picture, remembering about the shadows.

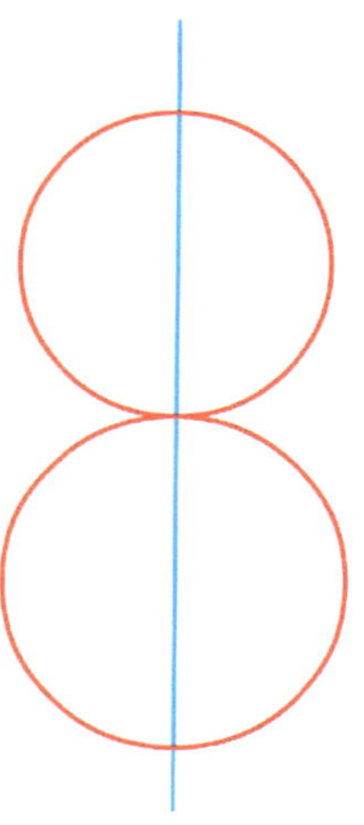

1. We start by drawing a simple auxiliary line (blue). Next, we mark two circles (red) on the auxiliary line. Notice that the guide line crosses their centers. A bunny's head will be made from the upper circle and a body from the lower one.

2. In the second stage, at the height of joining two circles, draw a neck (blue). In the center of the head, using the auxiliary line, we sketch a circle. At the bottom of the torso we draw two ovals from which the bunny's legs will be made (green).

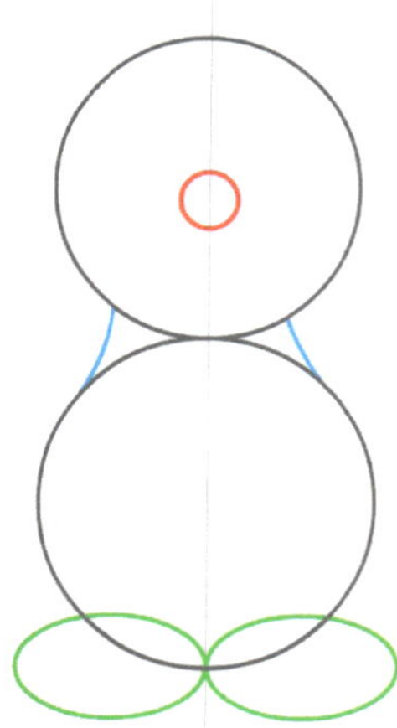

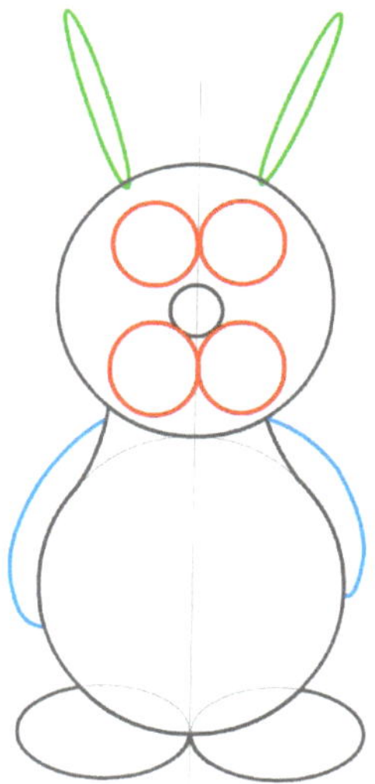

3. Now we can slightly erase unnecessary lines. With the help of two ovals, we sketch the ears (green). Then we draw four circles (red), from which the eyes and mouth will be formed. On the sides of the torso, sketch the outline of the paws (blue).

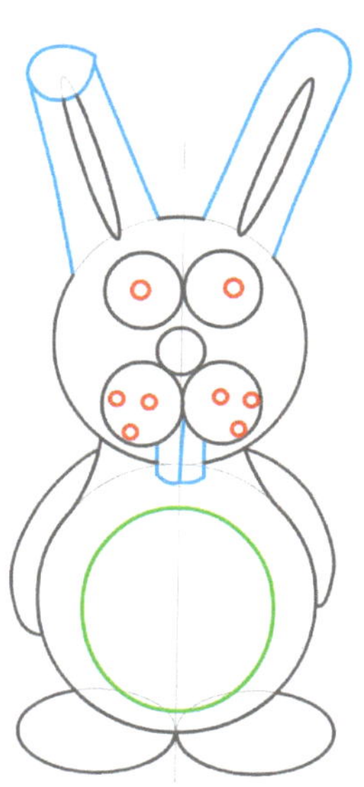

4. The next step is to sketch the outline of the ears and draw the teeth (blue). Then we put eight circles (red). In the middle of the body we draw an oval (green), from which the bunny's belly will be made.

5. At the end, erase all unnecessary auxiliary lines and correct the contours. Now color the drawing as shown in the picture, remembering about the shadows.